Drug I

Breiana Addison

Drug Of My Choice by *Breiana Addison*
Published by *ThroneRoom Expressions*
ThroneRoom Expressions Publishing Headquarters
33 Old Mill Lane
Southampton, PA 18966

©*2022 Breiana Addison.* All rights reserved. No part of this publication may be reproduced, stored in a retrieval system or transmitted in any form by any means, mechanical, electronic, photocopying, recording or otherwise – without the prior written permission of the author.

Cover Design by *ThroneRoom Expressions* & *Addison Graphics*
Editing by *ThroneRoom Expressions.*

For more information please contact:
ThroneRoom Expressions Publishing
throneroomexpressions@gmail.com.
info@charphelpsinternational.com
www.charphelpsinternational.com

Library of Congress Control Number: *2022922358S*
Printed in the United States

"And we know that God causes all things to work together for good to those who love God, to those who are called according to His purpose."
Romans 8:28

FOREWORD

Sometimes people go through life believing there aren't any choices. They tend to believe the pain they've endured throughout life is an indicator of the path they will continue to take. I can ensure you, that is not the case, and this book is a testament to that. Many of you may ask yourself, why should I read *Drug of My Choice*? Or maybe thinking to yourself, *healing* as a drug? How is that possible? Well, trauma has a way of changing us. It changes the way we think, feel, and behave, but so does *healing!* While trauma can consume every ounce of our lives, healing consumes every part of our existence.

When you are reading Brei's story, I implore you to not only see someone who continues to survive after trauma, but a person who continues to fight for her right of choice. Someone whose hard work has led her from looking at the world from fear and pain to faith and perseverance. We all have a journey; however, I encourage you to not only listen to her story, but to be reminded of yours as well. Regardless of where you are in your journey, know that you too have choice.

I cannot express how honored I am to be asked to write this foreword. How proud I am to be trusted with Breiana's journey. While these words may not do justice to what I feel and what I see in her, I will say this:

> In the wake of darkness there is light
> To be seen and to be shown
> A new life to be lived and experienced
> Even when the path is not known
> We may not know what will happen tomorrow
> Or forget about our lives of the past
> But there is room for now and today
> And healing will come at last

I am so proud you!

Love,
Dr. Ieshai Bailey-Davis, CMHC, LMHC, CST

Greison Jahmere Addison

"IF LOVE COULD HAVE SAVED YOU, YOU WOULD HAVE LIVED FOREVER!"

Sunrise
JUNE 9, 2014

Sunset
JULY 21, 2015

DEDICATION

To my sweet baby boy,
Greison Jahmere Addison (June 9, 2014 – July 21, 2015).
Thank you for being my greatest accomplishment. Your entrance changed me, and your exit fortified me. Although, I miss you with every fiber of my being, I understand daily a little bit more why it had to be this way. Mommy will always love you, Boogie.

To the greatest man I know, my husband, Willie.
Thank you for seeing the flawed me and loving without condition. You have been right by my side in the valley as well as on the mountain. .I couldn't imagine doing life with anyone else.
HappilyEverAddison, it's us against the world!
I love you more than words will ever be able to convey.

To the watchmen of my soul,
Apostle Ben & Dr. Kendra Carr-Pineda.
You saw me at my worst and somehow loved me in spite of it all. The words of encouragement and the rebukes motivated me to do be better. Thank you isn't enough, but I'll say it over and over again. I honor your pour. Thank you for your yes!
I love you all, always have, always will.

To my sounding board, Bishop Brian. P. Willis. Padre!
The way your role in my life has evolved has left me speechless.
Our bond is unbreakable, and I'll forever cherish it.
The random "I'm proud of you" text has healed me.
Your pour, prayers, push, and presence are forever etched in my heart.

I love you, Padre.

To the most amazing and solid support system, aka The Gang! My Mama, Nana, Nikki, Alfred, Latavia, Kendra, EP Kelle, Mother Melissa, Trystan, Justin, Tristan, Ebony, Char, and Charlene.
Thanks for wiping my tears and covering me while I recovered.
The invest you all have made in my life has sustained me. I love you all to life!

To the GOAT, my therapist, my vault!
Dr. Ieshai Bailey-Davis, CMHC, LMHC, CST.
I didn't know I needed you until I met you.
Thanks for assisting me in doing the framework.
Plenty of tears. Countless hours in session. An abundance of laughter. Solid Support. Unconditional love. Breakthrough prayers.
There aren't enough words to express my gratitude.
We stick to the plan no matter what! I love you, Eash.

INTRODUCTION

I've been struggling to find the right words or the strength to send a smoke signal but to no avail. My smile and ability to still show up has deceived many and caused all to miss my desperate cry for help. This has truly been the fight of my life and if tired was a person it would surely be me. I've never imagine becoming so tired with life until I entered this season.

Chaos can sometimes be the absence of discipline and submission. However, other times chaos is the result of ignorance. I come from a *"what happens in this house stays in this house"* and *"counseling is not for black people"* environment which caused me to navigate life with a muzzle on my mouth and a noose of fear around my neck. My heart and mind became a receptacle that only had the capacity to store trauma, grief, and life's disappointments. I was the epitome of the walking dead, but no one could see it beyond my ability to overextend myself for the betterment of others. Life was a struggle and seemingly I was losing it.

Fast forward now healing has become the latest trend, but no one speaks on how much work, transparency, and vulnerability that it requires to become the best version of yourself. However, I chose myself and decided to indulge in the journey of healing blindly and not fully understanding the sacrifices I would have to endure. Healing is an inside work with outside assistance. Choosing to heal meant losing all my shhhhh I'd held on to since I was 5 years old and becoming the person God has predestine me to be. I lost everything before and now I'm trying to secure the bag – I am the bag!

    Here is where I will remove my fig leaves and allow you a front row seat in my journey of self-discovery and healing, while offering you an opportunity to experience your own healing. In this book you will find parts of my story, epiphanies, scriptures, and prayers that caused me to be addicted to becoming whole. Healing hurts before it helps but the process is well worth the results. Healing is the ***Drug Of My Choice!***

CONTENTS

DEDICATION 7
INTRODUCTION 9
LETTER TO MY DAD 13
CHAPTER 1: MY DEALER 15
ADDICT PRAYERS 23
CHAPTER 2: FEENING 24
ADDICT PRAYERS 29
LETTER TO YOUNGER ME 30
CHAPTER 3: MY FIRST HIT 34
ADDICT PRAYERS 40
CHAPTER 4: STRUNG OUT 41
LETTER TO MY ABUSERS 50
CHAPTER 5: INTOXICATED 53
ADDICT PRAYERS 59
CHAPTER 6: OVERDOSE 60
LETTER TO MY HUSBAND 66
CHAPTER 7: RECOVERY 69
LETTER TO MY SWEET BOY 77
ADDICT PRAYERS 80

MEET THE AUTHOR.. 81

LETTER TO MY DAD

I never really thought I would be to the place where I would have to write a letter like this. However, before we dive too far into it, the one thing I need you to know is I love you more than anything, and I miss you more than words can ever express. The one thing I wish you would've done was prepare me to live life without my superhero, but one thing remains true. You were my superhero in life and you're still my superhero in death.

There's a constant war going on in my mind, because I know if you were still here things would've been so different. When you left me, my life went from being a fairytale to being pure survival mode. As far as I could see, you were the glue that held our family together. It wasn't really a thing then, but truly you were the *G.O.A.T.* For the longest I was so angry with you, because for the life of me, I couldn't understand why you chose to leave me here. I've endured so much and the only thing I've ever long for was for you to reassure me like you always did.

This world is cruel, and I definitely feel unprepared. My innocence was taken, you didn't get a chance to see me gradate, you didn't get a chance to walk me down the aisle and marry the love of my life. You didn't get a chance to see me have my first child nor will you ever get to see the woman I've become. However, it always does my heart some good when I hear people say you look just like your dad, or your dad would be so proud of you.

Dad, you gave me the best five years of my life. Even in that short amount of time you taught me the value of family, the importance of having good character, and the endless possibilities you could have with a good work ethic. Every major moment in my life I always pause and reflect on you and my kid. I'm working tirelessly to build an inheritance and leave a legacy that will always keep your name alive.

Just in case you never heard it I'm proud of you and I'm proud to be your daughter. I understand now you had no control over your exit, but it was all a part of God's plan. Thank you for being the best dad a girl like me could ever ask for. I hope I'm making you proud and I love you forever and always.

Love you forever,
Butt

CHAPTER 1: MY DEALER

> *"Make today's solid ground out of yesterday's quicksand." -Mos Def*

Imagine trying to build your entire life including family, friends, faith, career, and identity on quicksand. I, like many others, believed in fairy tales and I was certain that my life would mirror the perfect Disney movie without ever having to face adversities but boy, was I wrong. My foundation started off with my immediate family, my mom, my dad, my sister (which is nine years older than me) and myself. Everything I knew involved these three people, they were the perfectly imperfect people to teach me core values and how to survive in this *"dog eat dog"* world. With them, I was protected and loved, I never fathomed having to do life without either one of them.

Growing up we lived in a neighbor where drugs and violence was almost nonexistent. In fact, almost everyone around me didn't look like me. Most families were a part of the military so many of my friends came and went, and it became very hard for me to have constant and consistent friendships. However, just like everything else, the only constant thing around me was change! Soon after, the neighborhood became invested with drugs and violence. My days for going outside to play and enjoy childhood were over and the only option was staying in the house for my safety and to protect my innocence.

My mother worked her behind off to provide the best life she could for my sister and I, which meant often my sister stepped in and played the role of a second mother to me. The age difference and my inability to see things from her vantage point meant we bumped heads all the time. We fought like cats and dogs but the only thing we wanted from each other was to be understood. Although I adored my mom and my sister, my dad was my entire world. My daddy was my hero. Not only did he take care of my siblings and I, but he took care of many of the kids in our neighborhood. No one went without and he had his own way of making everyone feel special. The greatest moment every day of my life was him reminding me that I was his *"princess"* or his *"Butt"* which simply mean I was his last child.

If there was struggle, I never knew it because my parents did everything in their power to shelter me. Anything I could think about having they provided it whether it was the latest LiteBright or EasyBaked Oven. Seeing and being with my dad was like a breath of fresh air and I guess you could say I was the true definition of a *"daddy's girl!"* After all, I had him wrapped around my finger and even at a young age, I knew it. Although my mother and sister were very active in my life, my dad seem to be the star. I loved my mom, and I idolized my sister, but every opportunity I got to spend time with my dad, I did! Maybe it was because he was my protector, maybe it was because he loved me unconditionally, maybe it was because I was spoiled, and he gave me whatever I wanted. Whatever the reason was, my dad was always my go-to person.

"Man, who is born of a woman, Is short-lived and full of turmoil." Job 14:1 AMP

In those days, my life seemed so perfect. However, when do you begin to teach a child that life isn't a bed of roses? The signs were all around me, but at the age of 5, who teaches you how to read between the lines? At the age of 5, who teaches you about instinct? I didn't know what was going on, I just knew that I wanted to spend *all* my time with my dad. I felt like everyone else could wait and they would be there later. Little did I know that was a true statement. I wasn't prepared for the plot twist that I would soon experience.

On April 3, 1996, my life change and I lost my security blanket! I can remember the day as if it was yesterday or early this morning. That's how vivid the day is in my memory. My mom had to be to work at five in the morning and I can remember her stopping by my room where my daddy and I were asleep. She reminded him that she would be back after her doctor's appointment at 10:00 that morning. My mom left for work and now it was only my daddy, my sister, and I left in the house. My mom called back to the house around 7:56 am to tell my sister and I to get up and get dressed and also for my sister to fix my dad something to eat so he would be ready for his appointment. Please don't forget that I said my mom and dad had a conversation before she left for work.

    My sister began fixing breakfast after she combed my hair. I hated getting my hair combed but this morning it wasn't a fight as she gave me three ponytails and I was as happy as I could be. While my sister fixed the plates, she sent me upstairs to get my daddy so he could eat breakfast and be ready by the time my mom had returned from work. I went upstairs and noticed he was on the floor, but at the age of 5 that didn't phase me. I put my best foot forward and did all I could to wake my dad, but I was unsuccessful. I ran back downstairs, and I explained to my sister that my dad was too sleepy, and he did want to wake up.

Not knowing exactly what was going on, my sister sent me back upstairs but this time she told me,

"If you don't wake your daddy up and tell him to come eat, you gonna get a whooping!" I was scared because there is a nine-year difference between us two, but nevertheless I tried again. My sister wasn't being mean, but my mom had stressed to her how important this appointment was, and she was only trying to obey my mom. This time I touch my dad, I begin to shake him and cry out, *"daddy, daddy, get up or I'm gonna get a whooping"* but still didn't move. I knew something was wrong because my dad always spared me from getting disciplined. In fact, he never whooped me himself. However, this time I noticed he was cold so I gathered all the blankets I could see and placed them on him. I even used my favorite fuzzy blanket that I never allowed anyone to touch. I knew how he hated being cold and how sometimes the cold would make his bones hurt extremely bad.

With tears in my eyes, I went back to my sister, but this time I knew there would be a consequence of not having my daddy with me. To ensure that I wouldn't get in trouble, my sister called my mom on her job and explain that I was unable to wake my dad up. She then ran up the stairs and as soon as she saw my dad, she let out a screech that pierced my soul. I had no clue what was going on. She ran next door and got my cousin who was in the Health Academy at her high school, and she recently learned how to check a pulse.

The two of them raced back upstairs and my cousin touched my dad's cold body but there was no pulse or no heartbeat. My daddy, my superhero was dead. They called 911 and my mom rushed home from work. She called my other siblings and everyone was in a panic. Instead of people explaining to me what was going on, they began to ask me what happened? How was I supposed to know, I was only five and life as I knew it changed in less than three hours. I was expected to know so many answers to questions I couldn't even comprehend. The only thing I knew in those moments was I *needed* my dad!

I wish I could tell you more but everything from that point on was a blur. When my dad passed away that's when the scales came off my eyes and I was able to see everything and everybody for who they really were. It was in that moment I initially felt like the black sheep; nothing felt the same. The image of the funeral home bringing his body down the stairs with a white sheet that had their logo on it will forever be etched in my mind. At least the guy was courteous as he stopped and said, *"Baby girl, would you like to kiss him one last time!"* His voice was raspy and borderline creepy, but at the time it sounded like an angel was speaking to me. I declined the offer and tears welled up in my eyes. The last thing I thought I would have to do is tell my daddy bye. I experienced one of my greatest losses and heartbreaks at the ripe age of 5.

In my opinion, I wasn't prepared to live without my dad. I wasn't prepared to experience life without my protector nor was I able to comprehend the magnitude of heartache I would have to endure for the rest of my life. In those moments I met maturity and was forced to grow up in ways that no child should have to. Unfortunately, my dad's death costed me my entire childhood. No Father-Daughter dances, he wasn't there to intimidate my first boyfriend or girlfriend (I'll explain later), he wouldn't be there to walk me down the aisle, he wouldn't meet his grandchildren, and the list continues. I just wasn't prepared to live without him.

ADDICT PRAYERS
Prayers that provided comfort while on the journey to healing.

God, right now I don't understand why you keep taking the people away that mean the most to me. Death seems so unfair especially when I didn't have a chance to create all the memories I wanted to.

I'm mad, hurt, confused, and sad. Help me to understand your will and please soothe my heart. Dry my tears and help me get through these dark moments. God, I don't like what I am feeling but I trust you will see me through.

Amen.

Romans 14:8
If we live, we live for the Lord; and if we die, we die for the Lord. So, whether we live or die, we belong to the Lord.

CHAPTER 2: FEENING

There are times when things are extremely intense to the point where it's hard to think when pain has a way of speaking louder than your faith – if you allow it. The hardest thing to do is to attempt to heal from hurt that you try to hide for so long. For me, I couldn't understand the strength in being vulnerable because the trauma I endured caused me to always have a hard exterior. To everyone else I'm the strong go to person, but on the inside, I was just a broken little girl desperately needing and craving unconditional love, support and validation.

My dad's death crushed me to my core and I didn't know how to move forward, nor did I know how to voice the pain I was feeling inside. But it showed up in every interaction and relationship even as a child. I was mad as hell and without a doubt I wanted others to share in my pain. All through elementary school I had a behavior problem. It was nothing for me to do my work and then show my tail. Throwing chairs, flipping over desks, hitting teachers, fighting classmates, disturbing instruction time or nap time; anything you can think of I did. Not that I am proud of it in anyway but I was a little terrorist and no one even cared enough to get to the root.

Grief is a universal language! The trauma of finding my dad deceased without anyone properly explaining to me what was going on was the beginning of *unresolved grief.* We often only associate grief with the death of a person, but grief is experienced every time we lose something or someone we expected to always have. The process of grief is often inconsiderate, which is why it's important to have adequate coping skills. Its mandatory to give yourself grace to grieve!

I discovered grief is the vehicle that carries a multiplicity of emotions and feelings. Some are easily identified while others we are unable to explain, yet the pain runs deep. When you become speechless everything you feel has an odd way of showing up as a pain in your body. I couldn't explain what I was feeling, the only thing I knew was I was mad as hell. I was mad at everyone, including God! It didn't seem fair and I desperately needed answers.

The greatest obstacle I entered at this point was trying to figure out how to find the answers. Where was I going to go? Who was I going to ask? What was I going to ask? However, even after that, the bigger question was would any of those answers suffice or heal me? My soul was hurting. Whenever you encounter any lost that shifts your life you have to be willing to make an exchange so you won't become stagnate or end up on a downward spiral mentally, emotionally, physically or spiritually. I didn't know this then, so instead of releasing, I carried and suppressed everything.

There in nothing to fear in expressing emotions; the fear should be in consequences of suppression.

I began to be intrigued with living of the edge and taking risks even if that meant putting myself in harm's way. By the time I reached fifth grade, my attitude towards life was horrible. The only constant thing around me was change, and clearly, I was changing. My goal was to die to be with my dad but I just didn't know how it was going to happen. I submerged myself in church and community to activities, while secretly devising a plan to fulfill my craving. I was feening for something different and I was going to get it by any means necessary. It was clear I didn't have control over my dad's death. It was clear that I didn't have control over this next phase of my life, but I was definitely determined to gain some control. Although it's a clear contradiction, pain seemed to be the only thing I was comfortable with and I needed it to survive.

Whether people admit it or not, it's easy to continue to rehearse pain and nurture the feelings accompanied with it. I've spent the majority of my life being miserable in my own skin. So many days I would daydream about being someone else; fictional characters as well as those who appeared to have life all together. Contrary to my actions of attempting to push people away, I didn't want to be left alone because I needed someone to see past the mask and façade I had mastered. Did anyone see me?

Subconsciously I'd already counted myself out and unworthy of anything good based off a few minor situations. However, none of that would remotely compare to what I was about to experience soon. I was too young and naïve to understand that life doesn't stop happening because you're young and fragile. If anything, it seems like the fight intensifies to fortify you. I didn't know if I wanted to indulge in more pain or experience my first hit of healing. But the thought of doing something new terrified me, so I chose to stick with what I knew. I was feening for what was convenient and decided to get comfortable with the very thing that was ripping me apart –pain.

ADDICT PRAYERS

Prayers that provided comfort while on the journey to healing.

Father, I don't have all the right words, so I'll just pour out my heart to You. I don't know who I am anymore. I don't know why I feel the way that I feel. One moment I'm okay and the next I'm not. It seems like my bad days are outnumbering my good days.

I feel trapped in this place of helplessness and despair. Some days I wake up and I don't have the strength or the will power to get out of the bed. God, why did you allow me to live to see this day?

Is anything good going to come out of this day? I need your strength to make it through today. If you don't strengthen me, then I will fall. Your word says that you are near to them who are broken-hearted. Father, I'm broken. Please fix me? Make me whole again. Amen.

Psalms 34:17-18 NIV
"The righteous cry out, and the LORD hears them; he delivers them from all their troubles. The LORD is close to the brokenhearted and saves those who are crushed in spirit."

LETTER TO YOUNGER ME

Dear BreBre,

    I apologize! I put so much pressure on you to be strong and never show signs of weakness. However, the truth is there is so much strength in being vulnerable. In fact, being vulnerable is one of the most valuable characteristics you can possess. I understand now that your attitude was just a way to protect your heart. Many will confuse your form of protection as being mean but don't allow their opinions to box you in; they don't know your story.

    Just in case no one else told you, you are so beautiful and you are loved. Right now, you may not be able to see it, but one day your kind, plus size and dark skin, will be a hot commodity. Learn now to embrace you and love yourself unconditionally. The abuse you endured, mentally, physically, emotionally, and sexually was not your fault. People make choices and at the end of the day, you were a child – an innocent child. I applaud how resilient you are and your willingness to bounce back when you had every reason to run and hide.

There's no mistake you can make that would cause you to be unlovable. I love you, flaws, and all. Although it may be difficult at times, learn to lean on your support system. Some of your choices may be coupled with regret, but every decision will shape you to become an amazing individual. Stop allowing fear to hinder you from achieving your dreams and goals. You are one dope person. I apologize for always comparing you to the next person. No one really knows the mental anguish you have endured because you have suppressed it so well. Take a minute to breathe. It gets better in the end.

Bre, it's ok not to be ok! In the darkest moments it's ok to ask for extra support. Mental and emotional battles have no respect of person and the best of them struggle even if they never say anything. Please, don't allow the pressures of life to weigh you down so much that you feel like the only option is to end your life. Speak up and ask for what you need. Others may have similar experiences, but no one will ever be inside your body to know exactly what you feel. Don't fall prey to the stigma, choosing you is the most important decision you can make.

You cannot depend on others to adjust your crown. Life will knock the wind out of you but put your hands above your head and catch your breath. Inhale, Exhale! You must learn to pick yourself up even when you are in the darkest moments of life. You deserve the same love, compassion, encouragement, and push you give to others so effortlessly. Don't give yourself the short end of the stick. Despite the odds, you hold your head high and keep trying. Falling is a mistake, staying down is choice, choose to get up every time no matter how many times you fall. Don't you dare give up on you.

More than anything I want you to learn how to forgive and set proper boundaries. I know that certain situations and people have caused you to experience disappointments but learn to forgive quickly. Harvesting unforgiveness in your heart creates so many issues and if you are not careful you will feel the effects physically and mentally. Undoubtedly, unforgiveness can turn into resentment and rage and those are two things I would much rather you not have to deal with. The key to it all is to teach people how to treat you. No is a complete sentence; you don't have to offer an explanation. Boundaries should be one of the governing factors of your life no matter the area or person, you need boundaries Bre.

The possibilities are endless, and the world is yours. You will make an impact and leave an imprint. Your path will not be the same as others, it's not supposed to be. The most detrimental thing you can do is try to emulate someone's else journey. It might not make sense now, but one day you will learn to value the words, *"stick to the plan."* It's more people for you than against so buckle up, this will be one interesting, yet fulfilling journey.

CHAPTER 3: MY FIRST HIT

Entering middle school, the change of scenery should've brought on a change. I thought my plight would change since I went to the only magnet middle school in the city with such an amazing curriculum that would only cultivate the creative within. I thought it would be a fresh start because of the possibilities of creating new friendships and a new version of myself. I thought it would be different and I would no longer feen for pain. One thing I didn't know was it's impossible to change or move forward without dealing with the things you've swept under the rug.

The first day of sixth grade will forever be etched in my mind. It started out as a good day but quickly took a turn. What kid isn't excited and nervous on the first day of school? Unfortunately, it all got the best of me. Halfway through the day I fell asleep, but not just a light sleep, I was knocked out. My homeroom teacher attempted to wake me up but a burst of anger overcame me to the point it caused a scene. It was that day I met the guidance counselor. Due to the population of the school being under 350 students we didn't have deans. It was the guidance counselor that handled behavior issues as well as emotional support.

The first day at a new school and already I revealed a side of me I was trying so desperately to hide. Embarrassed is an understatement! When I become overwhelmed it's hard for me to articulate how I feel which results in me crying uncontrollably and that's exactly what happened. I cried because I didn't mean to fall asleep, nor did I mean to lose my composure. Contrary to what I felt, both my teacher and guidance counselor was only trying to help me and reassure me that this transition wouldn't be so bad.

    Nevertheless, the next day I was determined to start over and work twice as hard to focus and suppress what was consuming me. If I could be honest, what was bothering me was the very thing that introduced me to my drug. I was missing my dad tremendously. The pain of him not being with me was finally controlling me. My heart was broken in a million pieces and the only person I wanted to comfort me was my dad. The void of his presence and protection was paralyzing me. I didn't want to move on! I finally was regretting not seeing him when the funeral home attendant carried him out the house. I was regretting not going to the funeral because in my heart, seeing him one more time would provide more comfort than I could never explain.

    In front of others, I tried to drown out what I was feeling, but behind closed doors I overindulged in my pain. It was in my pain I felt closer to my dad, so I dwelled there.

At school, I had found my tribe, trauma bonding at its finest, yet we had an amazing bond. Somehow, I was able to connect with Krys more than the others. She understood the art of suppression and unbeknownst to everyone else, she had a pretty rough home life. Her mom was addicted to drugs, her sister treated her like an outcast, but her dad was her peace. He did everything in his power to protect her and obviously that reminded me of my dad. Due of the ongoing chaos she endured, she had her own secret. Krys, struggled with bulimia as well as cutting. It was her way of coping with her pain.

The more I spent time with Krys and the more we talked, it became easier for me to express the emptiness and loneliness that I felt daily. I finally found the courage to tell her that I dream about dying; the suicidal thoughts were running rampant. As a child, I heard several conversations that referenced suicide, it was always looked at in a negative light. *"So and so killed themselves,"* is what people would whisper. Suicide was always referred to as a *"rich white person's problem"* which made it difficult for me to express my battle. With Krys, I felt safe I'd learn to trust her with the most fragile parts of me. She didn't judge me, in fact to my surprise, she shared she too struggle with suicidal thoughts.

Never did I imagine finding someone who was just like me. When two people hang out one thing for sure is going to happen, either you're going to influence someone or they're going to influence you and this situation was no different. After having an extremely rough day I confided in Krys and the unthinkable happened. I wanted to feel something other than what was consuming and it was that day she introduced me to cutting. Walking the track at Encore, we decided to have a seat in the far corner away from everyone else. We were working on a symposium project and Krys just happened to have a pair of scissors in her pocket. I watched as she found the perfect spot on her stomach that could be concealed by a stretch mark and ever so gently but with a steady hand, she did it. Initially, it didn't seem real but once I saw the blood, I knew it was real.

I'd never been one to back down from a challenge nor was I the person who openly admitted when I was afraid. Krys basically gave me an in-person tutorial and now it was my turn. She handed me the scissors and I follow her steps by step guide, but when it was time to do it, my stomach was filled with butterflies. *"Go ahead and just do it. I was nervous the first time, but it took the pain away."* Her encouragement pushed me over the edge, and I did it. It was as quick as a finger prick, yet those few seconds felt like an eternity. My mind shifted from what I was dealing with from earlier and now I felt something new; I was numb. She taught me how to nurse my wounds, we did our secret handshake, and returned to class in the nick of time.

    The healing process was rigorous, and it was a real job trying to hide it. Whenever I felt overwhelmed my go-to thing became cutting. Krys explain to me the ins and outs of it. I knew not to cut on my arms or anywhere visible, I knew not to do it multiple times in a day and I knew the importance of keeping the cuts clean to prevent infection. But one thing she never told me was how guilty you felt after the numbness wore off. Running from one type of pain caused me to create another pain. But I committed to it, I was strung out and so far, it had offered more comfort than anything else I tried.

ADDICT PRAYERS
Prayers that provided comfort while on the journey to healing.

Lord, I'm struggling mentally and emotionally. I hate how I feel. My life hurts. My heart aches. I feel like I've failed at life. I feel like I can't do this any longer. Honestly, I'm not even sure if I want to do this anymore.

Everywhere I turn, there's a reminder of something painful. HELP!!! Please rescue me from this pit of dispose despair. I'm clinging on to my belief in you. You're the only thing that I must have hope in. God help!
Amen.

Deuteronomy 31:8 NIV

"The LORD himself goes before you and will be with you; he will never leave you nor forsake you. Do not be afraid; do not be discouraged."

CHAPTER 4: STRUNG OUT

I was full steam ahead; I'd mastered a version of self-harm. My timing was impeccable and so far, no one knew about my horrid habit although there were a few times I almost got caught due to my carelessness. I'd move beyond just using scissors. Anything sharp was a contender, although my favorite utensil was a shaving razor. Krys, on the other hand attempt to overdose and was now in a mental health program in Lakeview. Ironically, the person who introduced me to this drug was no longer around.

      Initially I felt rejected and alone because the one person I confided in the most was gone and battling something that I couldn't help her with. A part of me felt guilty that I couldn't support and comfort her how she had done for me some many times in the past. I'd always prided myself on being loyal and showing up for others but this time I felt like I had failed. Even as a middle schooler, the pressures of life were weighing so heavy and more and more of my friends were suffering from depression, anxiety, and unfortunately suicidal thoughts. There weren't enough resources available to help us and oddly enough, we were expected to just *"get over it."*

      Nevertheless, I persisted! I found a way to pick myself up and realign myself with my other friends. My forever best friend, Tristan, filled in every space that Krys occupied plus so much more. There were still no words to describe the random low moments I would experience or the vast mood swings, but with my newfound *"coping skills"* and journaling I was able to gain my footing. I finally learned to love my middle school; after all there was no place like BBMS.

The moment I left my guard down I was comforted with opposition again. I just thought I was always clumsy, but the truth is it was something so deeper than my inability to stand on my own feet. My mom was concerned with all the accidents I was having and decided to get me seen. After a series of doctors' appointments and being referred to a specialist to run more tests, I was diagnosed with a bone deteriorating condition. I didn't understand exactly what that encompassed, but what I did know is my life was clearly shifting gears.

My only option to experience a normal life meant having surgery on both of my knees. I was fortunate to become a patient of the Shriner's Hospital because it was there I was able to see children who also had like conditions endure surgery and come out better than before. In a way it offered me hope because I was beyond scared.

The downfall to it was I wasn't able to cut to cope, nor did I have Tristan by my side because my surgeries took place in Tampa, FL. Having the surgery seem to be the least of my worries – it was recovery that changed the trajectory of my life.

My mobility was limited, and I needed assistance to do just about anything. Prior to my procedure, I would have to walk to the end of the street to catch the bus for school. It was there Tristan and I would meet to go to school. Although he didn't go to BBMS, we shared buses. My mama understood the difficulty of maintaining my normal routine and decided to get me door to door bus services. Meaning the school bus picked me up in front of my house and the aid would assist me on and off the bus and the same thing happened at school. This routine was extremely convenient as well as comfortable.

As hard as it was for to me admit it, I originally felt embarrassed and like a burden because I required so much assistance. Truth is it was no need to have a pity party because it was the only way for me to get to and from school and my mama and Tristan reassured me it was only temporary.

Due to the shortage of school bus drivers, just when I was getting use to the door-to-door service, I had to change buses. The range of emotions I experienced were insurmountable because once again I was experiencing another change. I didn't feel like I had any stability and that alone was troublesome. My first encounter with my new bus driver was oddly different. He greeted me like he knew me.

He was warm, welcoming, enthusiastic, and hilarious. The man made me laugh the moment he saw me hopping on my crutches. Due to the change, my mama was home on the first day and that's when all the dots were connected. My bus driver and my mama grew up together and were very familiar with each other's families. She told me,

"Oh I'm not worried about you; I know for a fact you're in good hands."

From that day on, everything seemed to fall into place. I had no worries and getting to and from school was a breeze. Since he was a *"family friend,"* I would always be the last person to be dropped off at home and he would help me into the house. This continued and at the same time my knees were healing which meant my mobility increased but I wasn't cleared by my doctor to participate in strenuous activities quite yet. The more time I spent on the bus, the more my bus driver got to know me. It's safe to say we developed our own bond, so much so, my mama made him one of my godfathers.

It was a lot to take in, up until this point he had proven to be a protector and only wanted the best for me. He slowly introduced me to different conversations about love and relationships. I was slightly naïve and sheltered so I didn't think deep into it, nor did I see a problem with it. I assumed it was his way of preparing me for what was to come. But one day it went too far. The one day, Tristan didn't come to my house after school, my life changed.

It was already a gloomy day and school was all over the place. It was crunch time, projects were due, essays were due, band competition was vastly approaching and I just wanted to go home and escape from the day. Instead of taking me home on the school bus, he finished the bus route and took me home in his car. To some that should've been a red flag, but for me it was the norm because he had done it countless times before. Usually, it would happen when my mama had cooked a big meal and he wanted to fix a plate of leftovers.

We pulled up to the house and instead of getting out the car right away, we had another conversation about love and relationships. The conversation eventually ended up on the topic of sex. He began to say, *"it's better to drive the boat before you buy it."* That's what he left me with. He gathered my things and helped me in the house. I used the key and went to the bathroom; I'd held my bladder for much of the afternoon because I hated using public restrooms. When I came out the bathroom, he was sitting on the couch stroking his manhood. Shocked and uneasy, I tried to retire to my room upstairs however, he invited me to sit next to him.

    I don't know if I was moving too slow or if I was moving at all, nevertheless, he came and got me out the hallway. He asked me to touch "it." He asked again, and finally his request turned into a demand. I knew it wasn't right, but I was also clueless about what to do. He slowly moved his hand under my shirt and onto my chest as he maneuvered on top of me. I asked him what he was doing, and he simply replied, *"I love you."* His hand went up my dress and the struggle began. Ultimately, he overpowered me. He forced himself in me and my innocence was taken in a matter of minutes. Those minutes seemed to last a lifetime. Before leaving he made sure I took a bath, and the couch was fixed. He said,

    "This stays between us, it won't hurt too much longer."

I had no words, only tears because my *"god-father"* had violated my body and there was nothing I could do about it.

The following day, I didn't go to school because I couldn't face him. I made up a lie about not feeling well and my mama believed me. She never asked what was wrong and I am grateful because I was clueless about what to tell her. Just because I didn't go to school, that didn't stop him from coming by to *"check"* on me. I don't ever recall being that nervous to talk to someone. He came bearing some of my favorite gifts and I'm sure it was a peace offering. I wish I could say it only happened one time, but it happened so much that it was no longer a fight and it felt normal. Although he apologized, I knew nothing would be the same moving forward. From that point on forcing myself to vomit after almost every meal and cutting were daily habits. I was trying to do everything in my power to make myself unattracted as well as numb.

ADDICT PRAYERS

Prayers that provided comfort while on the journey to healing.

God, help me. Help me to rest in you. I know that I'm not alone even when I feel lonely. Please be my comfort. Lord, help me to find and feel joy again. Help me to find pleasure in living life. Help me find the will to live again.

Your word says that you came that we might have life and life more abundantly. I want the abundant life that you've promised. Your word says that the joy of the Lord is my strength. Send your strength in the form of joy. I can't continue like this.

I'm depending on you.

Amen.

James 1:2 NIV
Consider it pure joy, my brothers and sisters, whenever you face trials of many kinds.

LETTER TO MY ABUSERS

I never thought I would find the courage to say anything to you or even write this letter, but the more I choose to heal the more I realize it's necessary. I spent majority of my life trying to figure out why me? How could you think it was remotely *ok* to take advantage of me? Because of your actions, I've questioned my existence and everything about me. I hate it and somehow someway I felt like what happened was my fault.

The times when I was most vulnerable, the times where I was trying to navigate through life, the times where I was just trying to make it make sense, you preyed on me. I've had to wrestle with public humiliation, private humiliation, guilt, shame, and ultimately feeling dehumanized. I am choosing not to play the blame game, but what I will say is, I was only a child. The audacity of you to take my innocence! I've spent countless of hours in the shower, trying to scrub off the nastiness you left on my soul. You violated my soul!

Rape, molestation and being fondled are all taboo and no one wants to talk about it, however more people have experienced it than I can even imagine. At one point I hated you, I wanted you to suffer, and to be honest with you

I wish you were dead. But on the other hand, I loved you, cared for you, and often wondered why this had to be the outcome. It took me years to understand that it was less about me and more about power and control. Not to sound funny, but I hope the nut was worth it.

These incidences left me scarred, battered, broken, confused, perplexed, baffled and I was left speechless. The tears no longer fell from my eyes, but my soul cried out constantly. It's no point of lying about it, I thought my life was ruined. I wanted to die, and I tried to act on my thoughts. It wasn't until I got into counseling that I even attempted to find the light at the end of the tunnel. Honestly, I am not sure if I found it or not, but I know I'm not where you left me.

I forgive you, all of you, for everything you've ever done to violate my body. I don't call you names because you're not worthy that much energy. I've allowed you to help me walk around in fear for so long. I've allowed you to dictate my self-worth, my self-esteem, and my beauty. I've allowed you to taunt me in my dreams, and in my relationships due to fear of the unknown. I choose me today! I choose to love me! I choose to protect me! But more importantly, I choose to release you!

Whether or not I ever get an explanation as to why or if I ever get an apology, you no longer have control over me. I'm recovering. I'm healing. I'm moving forward!

CHAPTER 5: INTOXICATED

Losing my innocence turned me into a different person. It awakened a part of me that I wasn't prepared to deal with. My identity was tainted and I was on a journey to find fulfillment and love by any means necessary. Krys, was back at school but she was different. She had discovered her love for women and now was a stud. I loved it. I loved her. Slowly but surely, I developed the biggest crush ever. Being with her was easy and I wanted to experience more than previously; I wanted more than just a friendship.

My body would respond every time she was around. Basic conversation turned into making plans for the future and I found myself drifting into her arms and her into my heart. Once again, she provided something different, an escape and I was living for every moment. The problem with it all was I was clueless about what I was doing or what to expect. I didn't know the ins and outs of the LGBTIA+ community, but I was willing to learn about it if it meant being accepted and loved without limits.

As quiet as it was kept, Krys and I became an item; she was my first girlfriend. She had a way of making everything that was wrong feel right. We spent every chance we could together and because we were so low-key no one really bothered us. That was until she found someone who looked better than me and someone who had more experience in being a girlfriend. My first heartbreak came from a girl that I had plan to spend the rest of my life with. We went from being an item to enemies overnight.

How could she be so vindictive? In my eyes, she was the epitome of a backstabber, and I was determined to get my lick back. Perhaps she forgot who I was but I wasted no time on moving forward. I found someone who was older and more experience too. I upped the score. She catered to me, spoiled me, and made me seem like a real big deal. With females I felt safe. I longed to be with her all the time and that's exactly what I did. I found someone else.

It was convenient because we both were considered *"church girls."* Somehow, we mastered looking innocent and it was easy to get away with wanting to be with one another. With her I was willing to risk it all and nothing was off limits. At school we flaunted who we were to each other and it caused a minor war between Krys and I. I was trying to play my cards right, but often I got caught up in the back and forth.

Truth is my heart was still hurt; I had no words to express the pain I felt inside. It was a struggle to function and depression was kicking my ass, but I chose to fall further and further into my new girlfriend's arms. Up until this point what I knew about sex was very shallow. Kissing got you pregnant, only a man could fully please you, and oral sex meant you were mature. Being raped and molested taught me that sex was forceful, it hurts, and that I didn't have a say in what happened. Nevertheless, I was confused about it all.

My new girlfriend had a point to prove. The more time we spent together the less control I had over myself. We went from holding hands, to kissing, and from kissing to making out. Eventually, things progressed until we were exploring each other's bodies. There were times I would lose all my inhibitions and each time she would introduce something different to me. For those moments everything felt right. We had superseded the level Krys and I were on. We were in a new place. The problem was I was felt so empty afterwards.

The more I played on the playground I found myself drifting further and further away from myself. It's a miserable feeling when you feel disconnected from yourself. But that wasn't enough for me to stop. Her love was addicting, her lifestyle was addicting, and I refuse to compromise how I was feeling even if it meant being lost emotionally. I was a pro at living a double lifestyle. No one in my immediate family knew about the "other" me. She literally became my idol.

I was beyond mesmerized by being in the relationship that I overlooked her abuse. Due to the age difference and her experience, she naturally was more dominant than I. I called it loved but truth is I was enslaved to her. Her temper was shorter than a grain of rice and it felt like I was always walking on eggshells when we weren't engaged in intimacy. She would yell, shove me in my face, grab me, choke me, and push me. I couldn't imagine losing her, so I dealt with the abuse silently. The reason for her becoming upset or triggered was always minute and I began to feel like I was a magnet for pain and abuse. Chaos felt normal and despite the many opportunities for me to escape.

I was intoxicated. My judgement was impaired, and my pride hindered me from asking for help. Her love was conditional and temporary and when we went our separate ways, I was numb. I did everything to regain my feeling for life, so it was nothing to jump in and out of relationships with males and females. Since I was considered the "fat" girl I have the privilege to do plenty of my dirt under the radar. Noone suspected me to be the hoe, but that was my truth. I lost respect for myself, I felt like I was damaged goods, and I became extremely hopeless. Compromise caused me to endure a full identity crisis.

ADDICT PRAYERS
Prayers that provided comfort while on the journey to healing.

God, I acknowledge and admit that I'm broken. I need healing in every aspect of my being. My mind needs healing. My body needs healing. My soul needs healing. Life's trauma has caused the way I view the world to be skewed. I no longer see the positive in anything.

Your word says that whatever I desire that I can ask. And when I pray that I should believe. God, I ask for total and complete healing. I believe in all my heart that you can and will do it because you are the only true and living God. Your word also declares that healing is the children's bread. I have the right to be healed.

I have Heaven's permission to be healed. I don't have to feel remorse for being healed. There's no guilt and shame in my healing. God, I commit to walking in healing daily. Thank You does your healing.

Amen

Matthew 11:28-30 (NIV)
"Come to me, all you who are weary and burdened, and I will give you rest. Take my yoke upon you and learn from me, for I am gentle and humble in heart, and you will find rest for your souls. For my yoke is easy and my burden is light."

CHAPTER 6: OVERDOSE

I wanted nothing more than to have a break from life's tests and trials. I was engulfed by depression, oppression, and suicidal thoughts. However, to save face, I continued through life full steam ahead struggling to understand who I was and exactly what I wanted. It felt like I was a magnet for pain. There were plenty of times I created self-inflicted wounds because I had become accustomed to thriving in pain.

Towering through high school, I did my best to fit in as well as be invisible at the same time. It was a struggle to maintain and no matter how hard I tried I couldn't seem to find my place. Things were completely different compared to middle school and I had nowhere to hide. My grades were up and down, sometimes more down than up. I found myself doing the bare minimum just to pass. My life lacked joy and happiness, yet I continued moving forward.

Despite what I was dealing with, my friends or should I say associates always felt comfortable coming to me with their woes. It's safe to say I basically started my own counseling practice. Whether it was something as small as a school problem or something major as sexual abuse or home life struggles, they knew it was safe for me. There were days I was on my last leg and barely making it myself, but I knew how to put that on the backburner to be there for them. Slowly but surely, I had grown in love with the need to be needed. I found comfort in being able to help everyone else even when my life was in shambles.

My nights were long, being everyone's "savior" would've been great if I didn't internalize everything. Plenty of nights I would have nightmares and eventually I became too afraid to go to sleep. However, none of that stopped me from showing up for others nor did it force me to ask for help. I didn't know it, but I was slowly killing myself with the inability to say no.

I managed to make it through high school, I was still being everyone else's savior, but I needed someone to rescue me. At church I was one way but in school, the broken version of me showed up daily. Things had gotten out of control; my best friend and I started drinking wine coolers every day. We had our routine down packed, get out of school, have a "neighborhood adult" buy a couple of wine coolers or Four Lokos from the corner store and have a *great* afternoon.

The only place I found "peace" was church. It was at church I begun to create another version of myself. I didn't know much about the bible, but I did know how to say whatever people wanted to hear. Every activity that I could get involved in, I did. Youth programs, singing, outreach, Bible bowls, dancing, and everything else in between. All of my free time was spent doing something church related. It's safe to say, I learned church and religion but my foundation of a true relationship with God was shaky.

It was easy to have random encounters with God. Those moments that I allowed my emotions to convict me was not enough to change me. One thing for certain was there was a call on my life! No one told me that just because you have a call on your life that doesn't mean you are exempted from trials. I kept experiencing hit after hit and I found myself in some rough situations. I had placed myself on such a pedestal that I allowed my pride to prevent me from seeing that I was self-destructing.

Now I was preaching, singing, and leading thousands of youths while not knowing from one minute to the next if I wanted to be with men or women, while drinking, still self-harming, and trying to find my way. There wasn't a light at the end of the tunnel. I couldn't bring myself to admit that I wasn't the person everyone thought I was, so I ran. I couldn't bear to stay in the same environment that was full of triggers and reminders of my past and pain.

The kicker was I didn't have a plan and it showed. I found myself in a relationship with a preacher who was a part of the same denomination as I was at the time. I for sure thought this was a "God" thing since I wanted nothing more than to leave Pensacola. After talking for only a few months, we both decided it was a "good" idea for me to move with him to pursue the "next" phase of our relationship. Without thinking twice, I took him up on his offer.

He presented himself to be God sent in the beginning and he did everything that I could've wanted him to do. I don't know if I was excited to be away from home or enjoying the thrill of being in a relationship with a preacher. Whatever it was, it caused me to ignore every red flag possible. All my things were packed, and I relocated to a new state determined to make life better for myself. He was older, experienced in life, a veteran, and a father; I thought this was my forever.

I'll admit we moved entirely too fast and the only thing I knew about him was what he told me but to my surprise everything was a lie. The preacher lied to me – imagine that! He was controlling, verbally and emotionally abusive, but to make things worse *he was married*. The man had a whole wife and everyone knew about her but me. For months, I was excited to be a clown because that's how I felt. This wasn't my idea of something new, I slowly begun to feel like everything I was running from back home had followed me to a different state.

    The breakup was one of the most embarrassing things I had to endure as an adult. It would have been okay if it only effected my natural life, but since he was a preacher it seemed like everyone knew our business. I was tired of explaining myself and regardless to how low I felt I refused to go back home. I was determined to make the best of the situation, so I enrolled in college and once again allowed church activities to consume me. At this point in my life, I'd given up on love and my ability to make sound decisions.

Everything I touched failed!

LETTER TO MY HUSBAND

My Love,

After all that I experienced in life I had given up on the fairytale of being married to my knight in shining armor. My life was in disarray and my heart was shattered. Honestly, I didn't think anybody wanted me. There is so much I had endured that I never spoke on, but it changed me and my ability to receive love.

I had concluded that I would either be single for the rest of my life or a hoe. Regardless to it all, I was going to make it work for me. When I met you, it wasn't my intentions to be with you. I was fresh out of a relationship. I was broken. I was mad at the church and I couldn't bear the thought of starting over. It takes so much work getting to know a person, but my greatest struggle was learning to trust and be vulnerable.

I felt invisible and to be honest I'm not sure how you noticed me but I'm grateful. You invited me to dance at your youth program but I didn't know I would have to use my nursing skills. One conversation to check on a sick church member turned into four hours of restoration. Somehow your charming ways massaged my heart and gave me a glimpse of hope. I've never gotten those crazy butterfly feelings before, but the silkiness of your voice and the tenderness of your heart changed all of that.

I didn't know how to love you and I didn't know how to appreciate you, but that didn't stop you from loving me. Together, we've shared some of our deepest secrets, our greatest highs, and lowest lows. You saw the broken little girl, the confused teenager, and the loss woman, but you became determined to help me find myself. It takes a strong man to repair a woman he didn't break.

When you asked me to marry you, I was excited yet scared. However, I've never been so confident in my life as I was when I said yes. Thank you for loving and growing with me and being the best part of me. Marriage isn't easy, but I wouldn't want to do it with anyone else.

Your prayers have rescued me, your leadership keeps me balanced, and your charm captivates me. You are the pillar in our family dynamics, and you hold us together. Even when you're having your moments you still manage to reassure me that everything is going to be OK.

It's because of you that I have a true foundation in God. It's because of you that I haven't given up. It's because of you that I can be a mommy to the most amazing kid there is. It's because of you that I'm pursuing my dreams. It's because of you that we are still standing.

If I don't ever tell you again, you will always have this proof. I love you more than words can express and I'm so grateful that you took a chance on loving me. I am so grateful that you took another chance at love. I'm so grateful to be Mrs. Willie J. Addison.

It's us against the world. I love you forever baby!

CHAPTER 7: RECOVERY

You can influence others, but you can't change them! The only person you have control over is yourself and that's limited when you totally yield yourself to God. It took forever for me to grasp this concept, but after losing myself time and time again and trying to fix me on my own, the only option I had was to rely on God. Slowly but surely, I started to relinquish myself back to God and everything I'd suppress since I was a child started to come up more and more. I didn't know how to handle it, after all I was still functioning on the *"what happens in this house stays in this house"* mentality.

Just when I became settled with being single, I met the man of my dreams. I found so much pleasure in dancing and teaching dance because it's where I felt most free and nothing seemed to be able to penetrate me in those moments. While teaching dance I had my first encounter with the man of my dreams. I wasn't looking to be with anyone and to let him tell it, neither was he. But through irony and sickness, we somehow made a connection.

In my mind I thought I had to be perfect before better would come to me. I wasn't expecting for my life to change while still trying to find my way through. I knew I wanted to be whole, but I also knew that I didn't want to be alone. Ever since I could remember I always dreamed about a happily ever after. One phone call changed the whole trajectory of my life. Willie invited me to his church to dance however, that service the speaker passes out as she was preparing to preach. Naturally, the church prayed but I couldn't allow her to lay there unconscious, all the skills I'd gain from health academy and college kicked in and I was able to assist her until helped arrived. The adrenaline kicked in and I wanted nothing more than to know she was going to be ok.

  Weeks passed by and I reached out to check on her since I hadn't heard anything. My person of contact just so happened to be Willie. One phone call to check on the speaker turned into a four hour conversation getting to know one another. We laughed, cried, shared dreams, and even shared fears all in our first conversation. How could this be, I felt like I'd known him all my life on one hand and on the other, he felt like the missing puzzle piece. I didn't know how to feel after our first conversation, but what I did know I was I couldn't wait until our next one.

  Every day from that first time we spent hours on the phone and eventually worked our way to going on dates with one another.

The dilemma was church as I didn't want to have a repeat of the last relationship. We chose to keep our business to ourselves and shared with very few people that we were dating. However, we did decide to pursue God together.

Things were different and for the first time in a relationship I felt safe. Somehow along the way, I'd become addicted to being loved correctly. If you really know, then to say I am afraid of animals is an understatement, yet he asked me to marry him at the aquarium. We were dated and married in nine months and to many peoples' surprise, I wasn't pregnant. Of course, many had their opinions but for the first time I begun to experience stability. Together we were a force to be reckoned with; perfectly imperfect.

Marriage presented challenges, but what do you expect when you have two people with different backgrounds coming together to build a life. Blood, sweat, and tears to say the least. However, we made up our minds that divorce wasn't an option, and we would be willing to work through anything. Clearly, we weren't prepared for *"anything."*

Our family begin to grow, our first pregnancy ended by miscarriage, and it placed a strain on our relationship. Although we both had experience loss in the past, this was our first one together. For whatever reason, God gave us another chance almost immediately, and I got pregnant with our beloved Greison. Young and full of excitement, we both couldn't wait to be parents. The doctors discovered he would have major health challenges and recommended me to terminate my pregnancy. In my heart I couldn't do it because I knew Greison would be our gift.

Greison was born premature and it was obvious we had an uphill battle, but we were both up for the challenge. We did everything in our power to ensure he had the greatest quality of life. Plenty of sleepless nights and countless doctors' appointments and we wanted nothing more than our baby boy to be healed. In just a short time we'd become real advocates for children disabilities because everyone deserved to be treated fairly. We saw life differently once we had him, but we still believed Greison was our gift.

As if our marriage hadn't taken enough hits, on July 21, 2015, at 5:34pm we took our biggest hit, our sweet boy transitioned. Neither one of us knew what to do or how to process life. Confusion, anger, rage, disappointment, and grief paralyzed us. We went from being a family of three to a family of two within a matter of minutes and there was nothing to comfort our hearts.

Depression caused both my husband and I to be functioning alcoholics and an isolated situation caused childhood trauma and life events to resurface in both of our lives. All sudden neither one of us were ok nor did we know how to adequately support one another. For me, I lost myself in being a caregiver and Willie lost himself in work. We went from living, to simply existing and it was completely miserable.

To the naked eye we were ok, but truth is we were falling completely apart. Gratefully someone finally saw us and forced us into counseling. I didn't realize how bad it had gotten until others begun to point out how we both would lash out and how we'd change completely. Those statements broke my heart because I didn't like who we've become but I didn't know it was affecting our relationships. Counseling was the best decision we'd ever made outside of marrying each other.

It was in counseling the little girl was exposed and forced to heal. Towering through emotion, heartache, flashbacks, abuse, abandonment, rejection, and being misunderstood became extremely overwhelming. Countless times I questioned God and asked him why I had to be the one to endure so much. After every session I wanted to quit. The emotional rollercoaster became too much to process. The more I unpacked situations the more things came to mind that I intentionally forgot. But the more I released the better I felt.

Healing requires commitment and so does change. After trying to fill the void I felt for so long, I knew the only thing left to do was take my first hit. Instantly, I felt nervous and unsure, but oddly excited. I was certain my life was about to change. Initially I was sneaking to indulge, but the high became too great to conceal. I'd experienced a pseudo high through guilt, shame, depression, and defeat and they only lasted for a moment. With every hit, the euphoric feeling increased and I knew there was no turning back. This drug was a game changer, and I'd easily became addicted. Healing never felt so good!

I made a promise to myself that I would no longer be addicted to rehearsing my pain or inflicting pain on myself. Instead, I would pursue being healed and whole with everything in me. Sometimes I feel like I am in the middle of Jumaji, but I have resolved that it would be worth it in the end.

Life happens differently for everyone, and I am determined to not to allow others to dictate how I heal. It's easy for someone to tell you how to heal when they haven't walked a mile in your shoes. However, I chose to be true to me. You can't heal from anything you won't confort. Being miserable in my own skin was no longer an option, I refuse to keep showing up for others while functioning on empty.

      Healing is a continuous journey and for the first time ever I am choosing me. I have survived things that would've have either killed others or caused them to be in a mental institution. One thing about it is you must make your mental health a priority and if you can get a handle on your mental health, your physical health will follow.
I haven't arrived and there is still more work to do, but I choose healing and the journey of healing from here on out. The right addiction will save your life, after all it saved mine.

LETTER TO MY SWEET BOY

Greison, you are so damn perfect! I don't know what I did to deserve such a perfect gift. I was so clueless when you came along, but I was willing to risk it all for you. Many looked at you and saw your large head, your cleft lip and palate but your dad and I saw a miracle. Your health challenges didn't define you. They made you special and to be honest, you saved our lives, and we're forever indebted to you.

All my life I've long for unconditional love, because for some reason, I always felt like I was unworthy. Boogie popped on the scene and taught me so many lessons that I didn't know I needed to learn. There are many days I wanted to give up, but I will look at you and see how you would endure despite the pain you felt and that along with motivation to keep going. Who would've thought a 6 pounds 2.8 ounces little boy would make such a huge impact on my life.

Your smile and charm gripped the hearts of everyone you met. You were quite the lady's man like your dad (might I add) and surely that was going to get you in trouble at some point. It's no secret that your health was extremely challenging, but at the same token, neither did the world know the strength you possessed. The first lesson you taught me was to smile regardless. I watched you have full seizures, and as soon as you finished, you smiled, and I never understood how you could do such a thing.

Boog, no one could give cuddles like you and the whole sloppy kisses, especially before your lip was repaired. You provided so much joy and comfort. The days I felt like I wasn't good enough you would grab me and hold me tight. The days I felt like I didn't protect you enough you would cling to me and not want to be bother with anyone else. The days I felt like I didn't know what I was doing you would go throughout the whole day laughing, giggling, and reassuring me that we were in this together. You meant the world to me and I never experienced a love like yours.

Your life became a testimony to me and example of God's love. Greison, thank you so much for loving mommy and giving me the chance to be a mother. My heart aches because every day I wish you were still here. I wish I had the opportunity to see you grow up in blossom into the brilliant young man I knew you would be. I remind myself daily that you completed your assignment here on earth which was to impact the hearts of many people. Honestly, I'm not sure if the world deserved you but please understand, I would fight a lion if that meant protecting you.

If love could've saved you, you would've lived for forever. I did my best to honor you and listen to your body language and your spirit. I made some hard decisions, but your dad and I refused to see you suffer. Our last conversation will forever be etched in my mind and heart. I reassured you that we will be ok and whatever you decided to do was well. Ultimately you and God had an appointment, and you chose to return home. Thank you, baby boy. Please continue to rest and know you are always alive in my heart.

It's not goodbye Boog, it's see you later. Forever, Greison!

ADDICT PRAYERS

Prayers that provided comfort while on the journey to healing.

Lord, thank you! Thank you for my life. Even when I don't understand I still thank you. Even when life gets hard, Thank You! Thank you for never leaving me even when I thought I was alone. Thank you for being my comfort in turmoil. Thank you for healing me through and through! Thank you for restoring me.
Thank you for holding me together when I was falling apart. Thank you for being God and giving me hope. I'll never be to say thank you enough, so I'll do everything within me to please you with my life.
Amen.

Colossians 4:2
In everything give thanks: for this is the will of God in Christ Jesus concerning you.

MEET THE AUTHOR

Conqueror. Creative. Called. Breiana Addison is a native of Pensacola, FL. She's the youngest child from both of her parents but has always displayed maturity beyond her years. Breiana has always had a passion for helping others and pursued the medical field in her high school and college studies. After working as a CAN and later an LPN, she realized that she wasn't feeling fulfilled and decided to embrace the creative within and explored the arts.

Breiana is married to Willie J. Addison, and they have one angel child, Greison. Her vivid imagination has led her to start a graphic design and branding company, Addison Graphics. Although she's self-taught, her gifts have presented opportunities to share her creativity throughout several states as well as the U.S. Virgin Islands.

The calling on her life is very great and it has led her to have a sincere desire to help youth as well as young women who often struggle with self-identity. Breiana embodies the characteristics of being an overcomer. Through faith and counseling, she has conquered things that were designed to kill her!

***2 Corinthians 12:9 NIV** "But he said to me, "My grace is sufficient for you, for my power is made perfect in weakness." Therefore, I will boast all the more gladly about my weaknesses, so that Christ's power may rest on me."*

Made in the USA
Columbia, SC
29 December 2022